"Stethoscope Dreams" Copyright 2022 by Dr. Wendy Goodall McDonald

First Paperback Edition September 2022

Written by Dr. Wendy Goodall McDonald

Illustrations by Nai Nyhan Saechao

Graphic Design by Rahsaan Taylor

ISBN 978-0-9993341-5-7

Published by Wendy Goodall McDonald M.D. via Kindle Direct Publishing

https://dreverywoman.com

This book is for all humans who love learning about how the body works.

A Note to the Reader

This book introduces the inner workings of all parts of the human body. It includes brief descriptions of the location and function of multiple organs, including the reproductive organs of humans with vaginas and penises.

Studies show that children who know the proper names and functions of organs grow up to live healthier lives and develop a love for science. I hope books like these foster healthy conversations about the human body with young readers.

The human body is so fascinating!

"Hi, Journie, my love. What are you reading?" said Mom.

"Oh, I'm just learning about the human body."

"Oh really? I love that. What made you want to learn about the human body?" said Mom.

Well, you know I'm going to be a DOCTOR, but I am also interested in how a human is forming in you right now.

"It is pretty fascinating. I know I deliver babies for a living, but the thought that our bodies can form other bodies is so awesome."

"What have you learned so far? What are the different body systems? Let's break it down!" said Mom

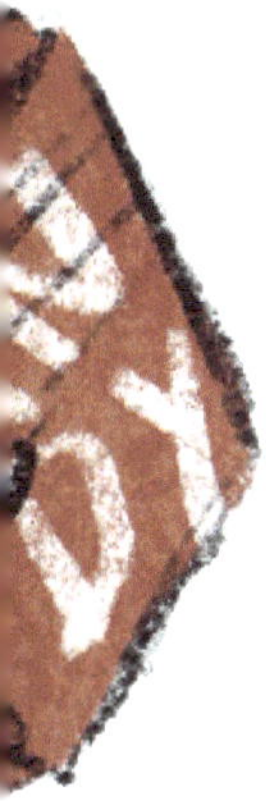

Oh, Breaking it down is what I doooo!!!

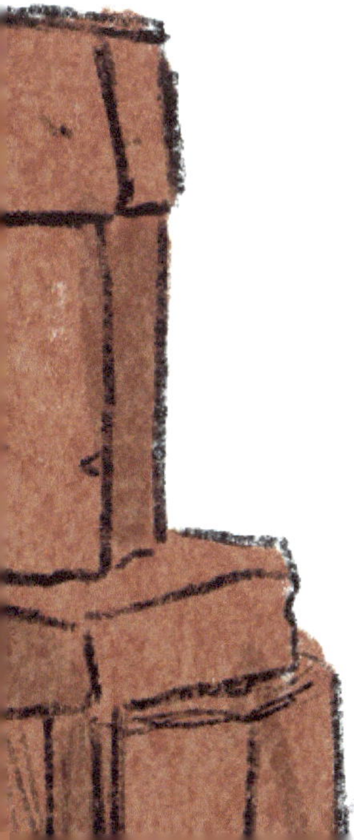

The skin is the body's largest organ.

The skin protects our body from bacteria, helps control our temperature, and protects us from chemicals.

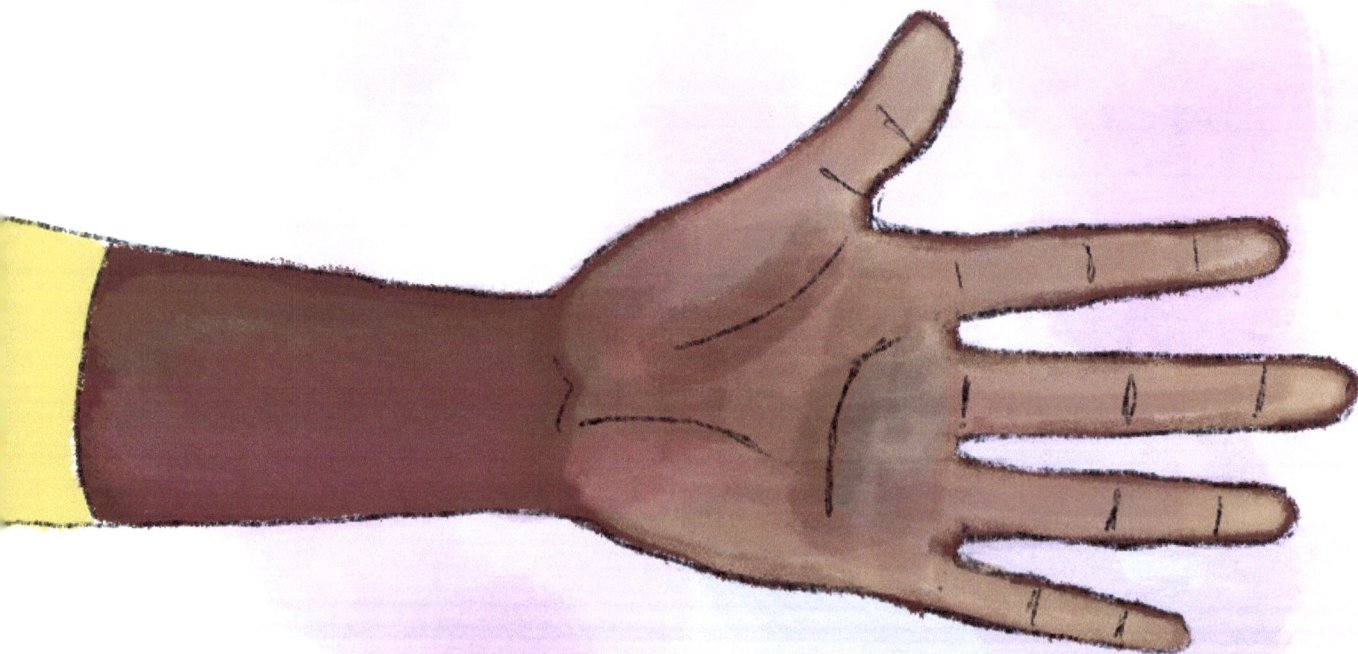

Skin is made of three layers- the epidermis, the dermis, and the hypodermis.

The epidermis (Eh-Pi-Derm-is) is the higher waterproof layer where our melanin lives.

The dermis (Derm-is) is the middle layer containing hair follicles and sweat glands.

The deeper tissue, also known as the hypodermis (Hi-Po-Derm-is), is mostly fat and connective tissue. Connective tissue connects tissue to other tissue.

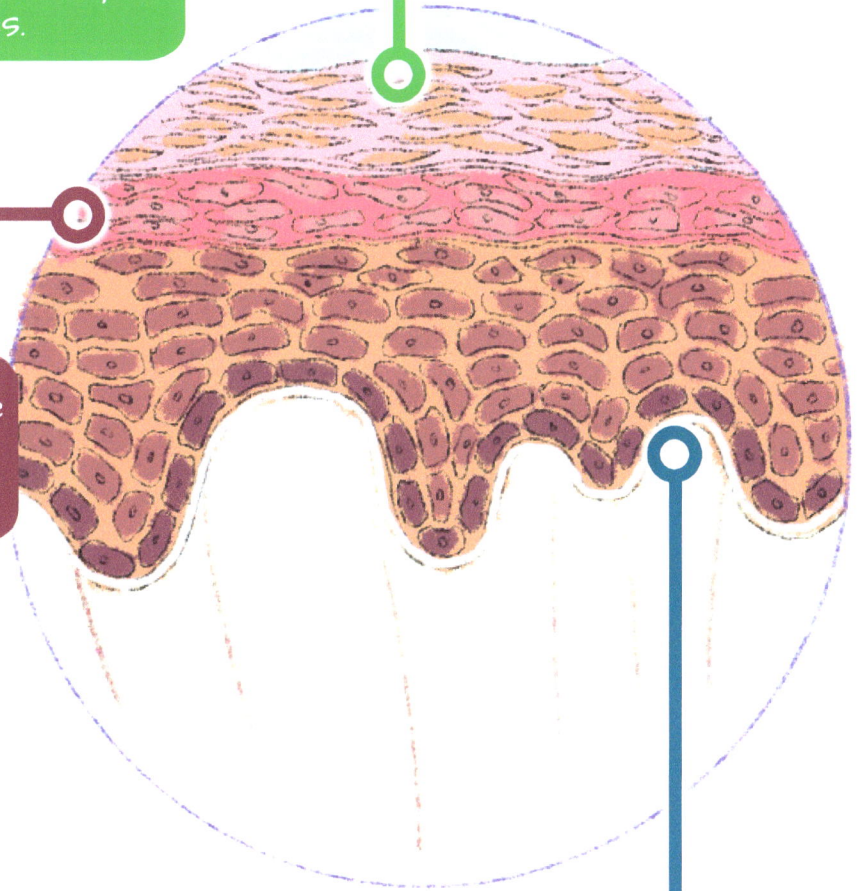

Our hair starts deep inside a
tiny tube called a hair follicle
and grows like a plant
with a root.

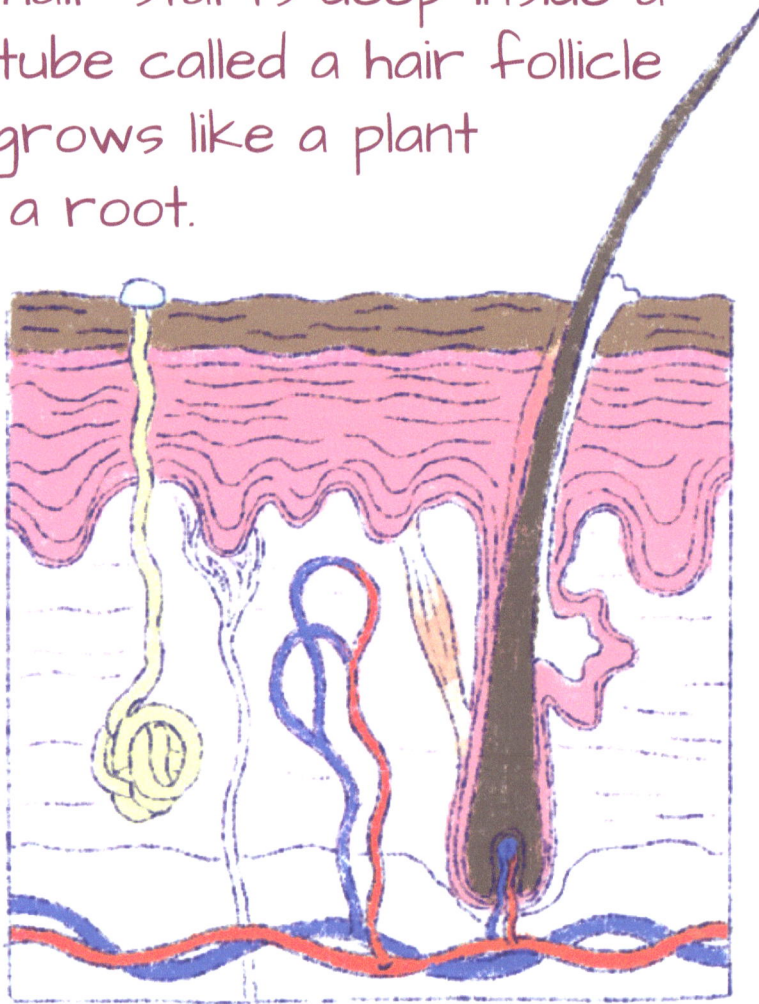

The root is under our skin.

When hair grows, it comes out of tiny holes in our skin. The shape of the hair follicle determines the texture or curl pattern of a person's hair. Your genes partly determine your follicle shape.

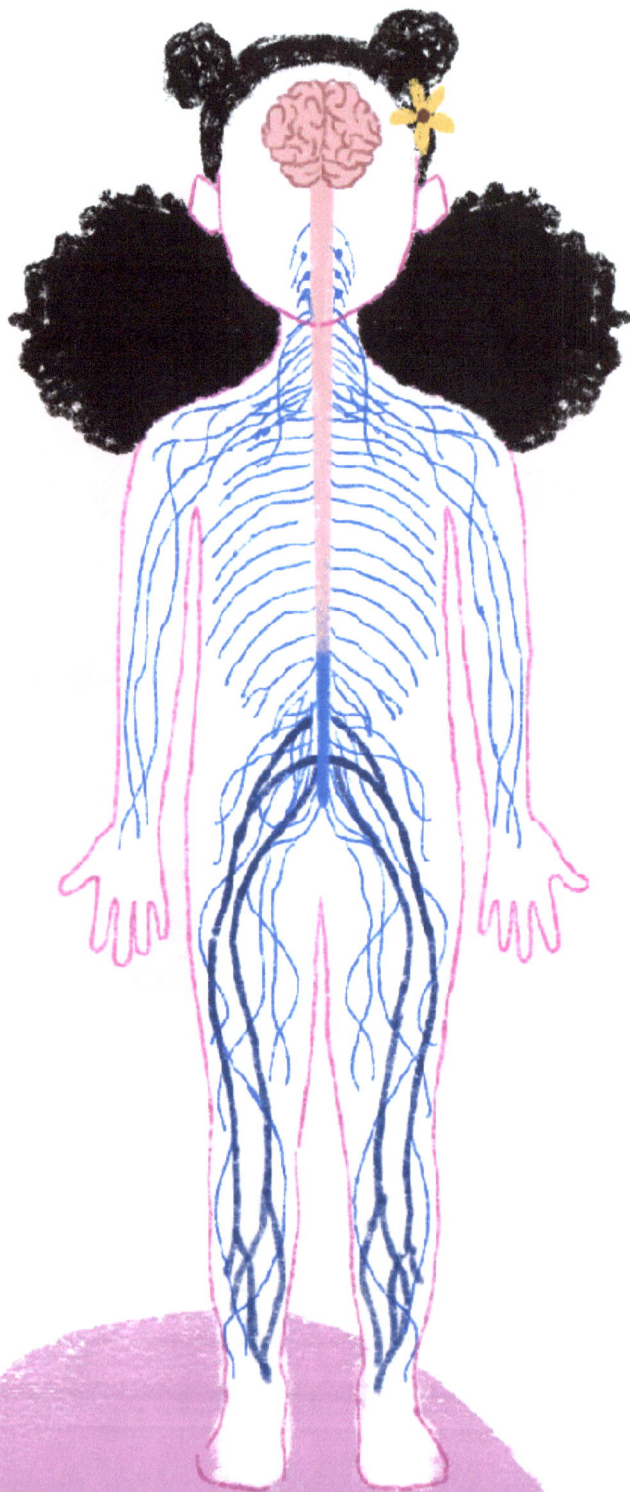

The brain is like the body's computer. It is what we use to think.

The spinal cord and nerves come from the base or bottom of the brain.

Nerves also send signals to our muscles when we want to move.

We use nerves to think, see, feel, smell, and taste.

The skeleton is all of our bones. They hold us up like wood in a tree.

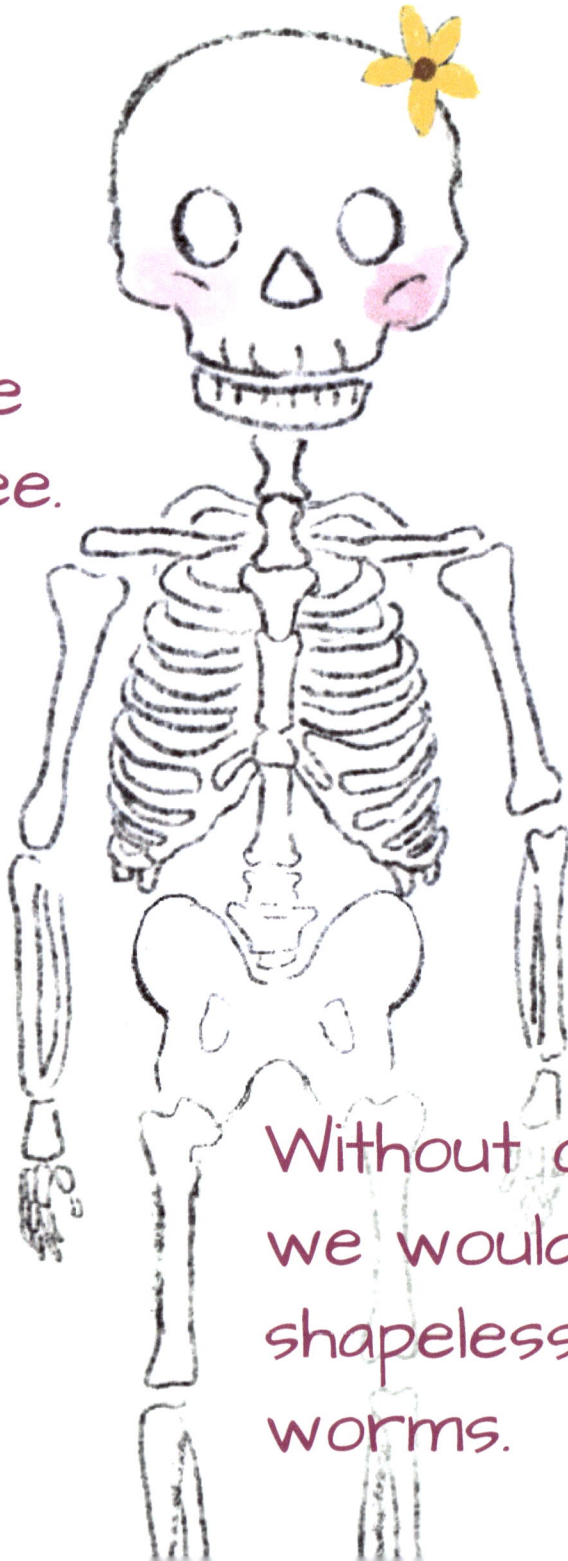

Without our bones, we would be shapeless blobs like worms.

Did you know that the largest bone in the body is in our leg, called the Femur? The smallest bone in the body is inside our ear, called the Stapes.

Our muscles help us move, breathe, exercise, pick up things, and even see.

"How do muscles help us see?" said Miles.

We have muscles on the sides of our eyes that make them move from side to side.

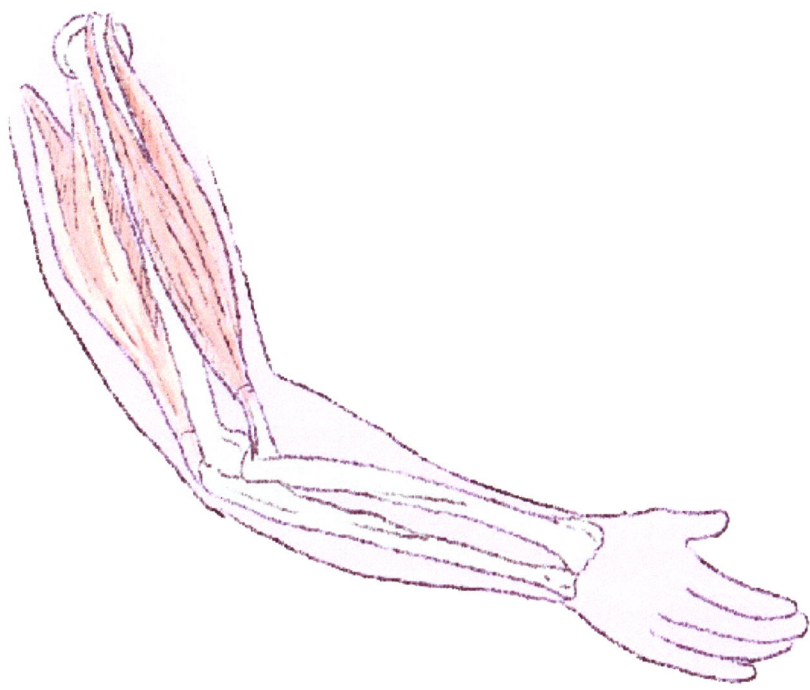

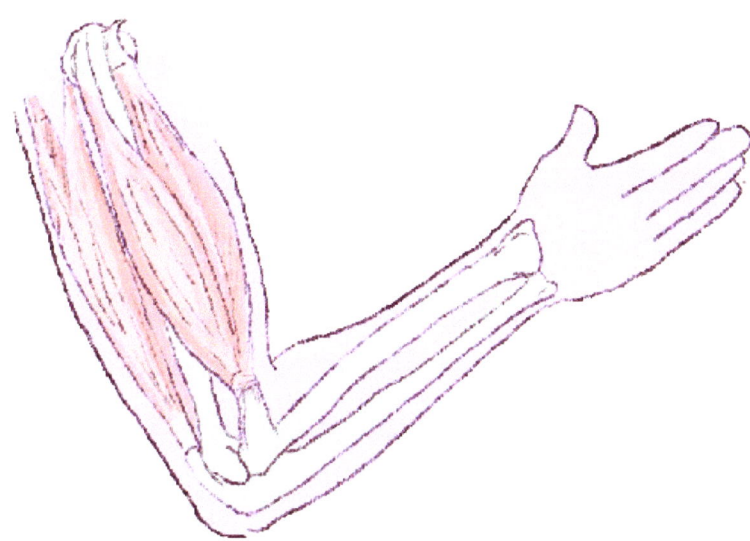

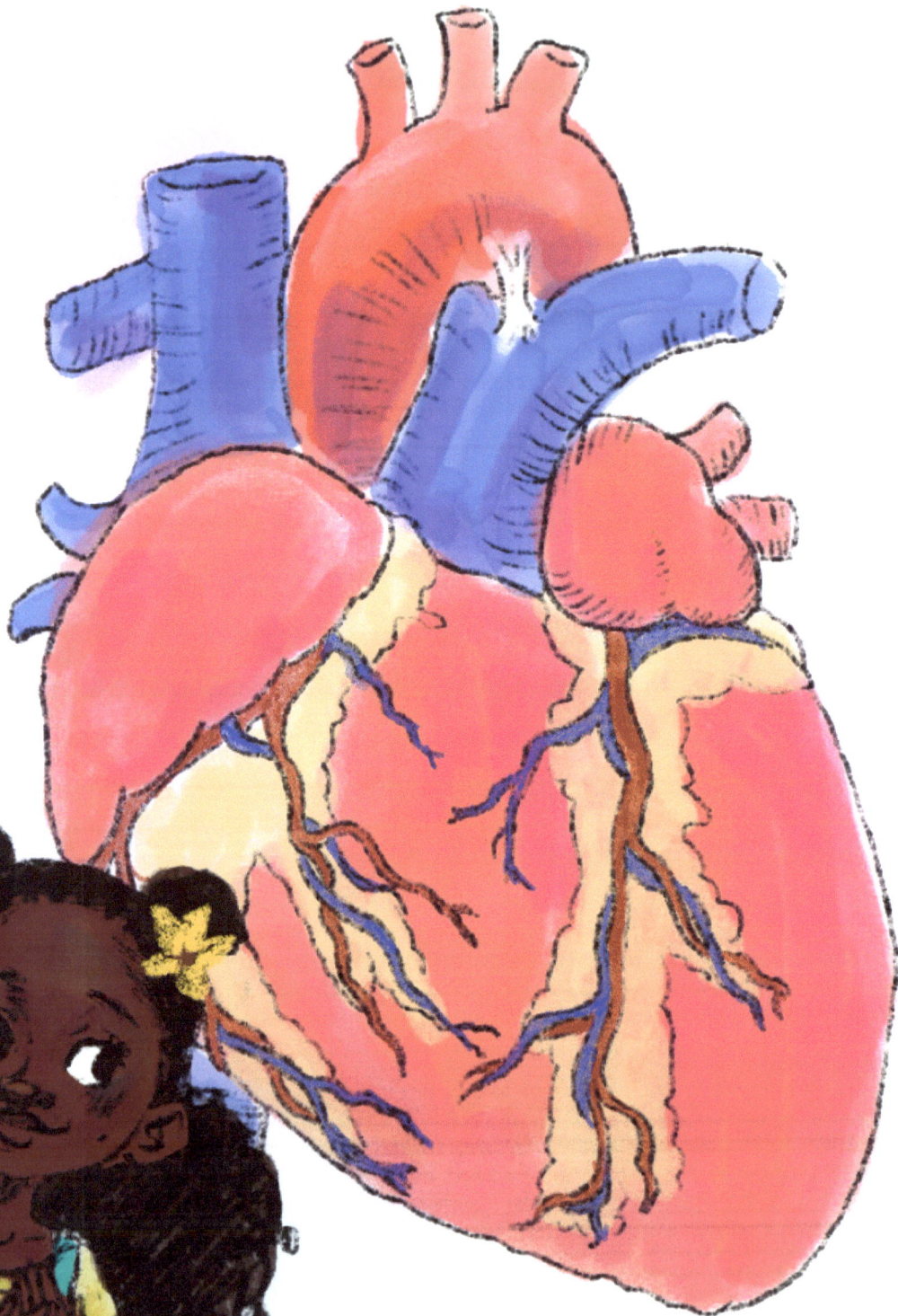

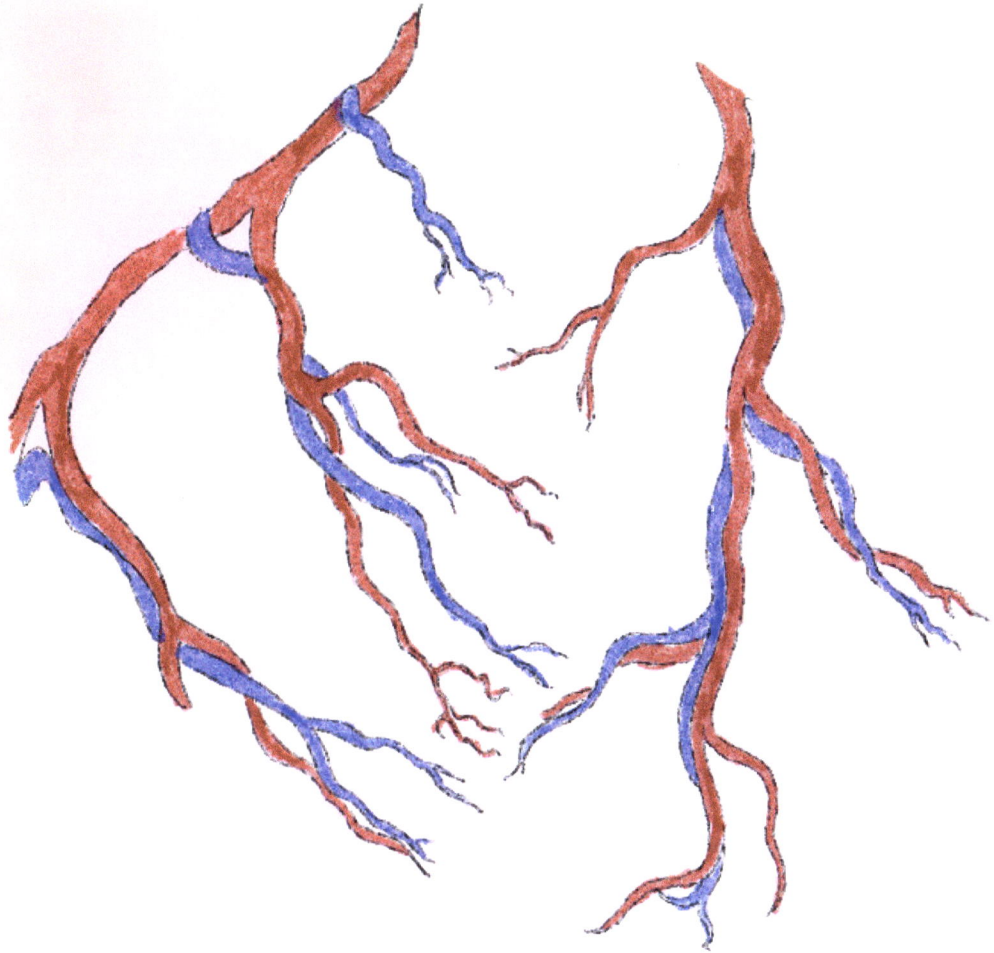

Our heart pumps blood throughout the body.

Arteries carry blood with oxygen to parts of our body that need it.

Veins bring blood that is low on oxygen back to get more oxygen from the lungs.

The lungs are where our blood fills up with oxygen that we breathe from the air.

The lungs are like an oxygen battery charger. The heart pumps uncharged or de-oxygenated blood to the lungs. The lungs charge the blood with oxygen, and that oxygenated blood goes back to the heart and pumps out to the rest of our body.

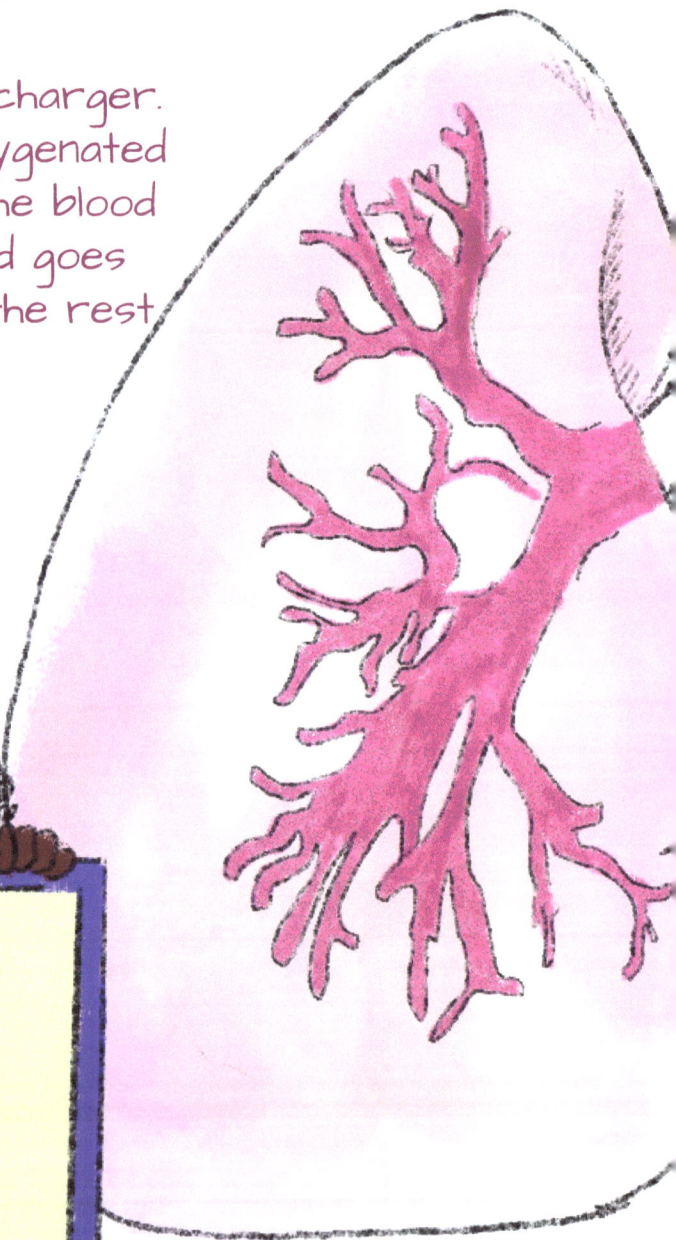

Air transfers oxygen to the blood in the alveoli.

Say it with me: Al-Vee-Oh-Lie.

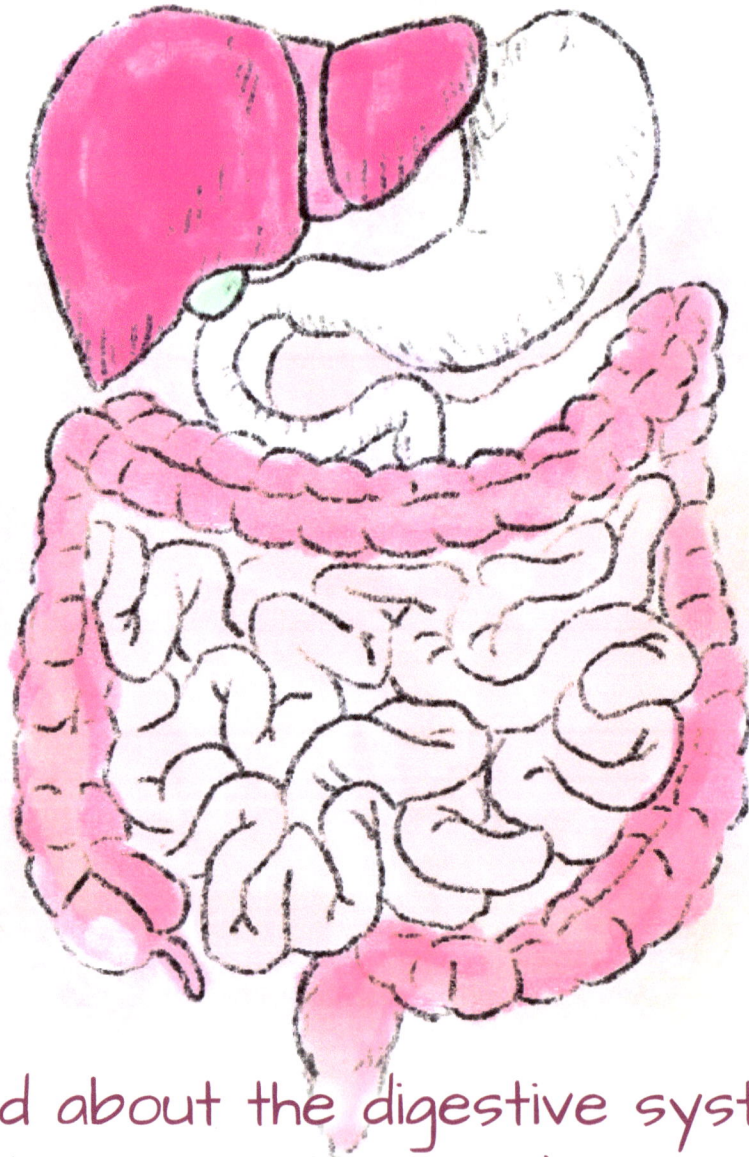

I learned about the digestive system from the book Do You Know Where My Food Goes?

When I eat food, it goes down a tube called the esophagus. It sounds like E-Sof-A-Gus.

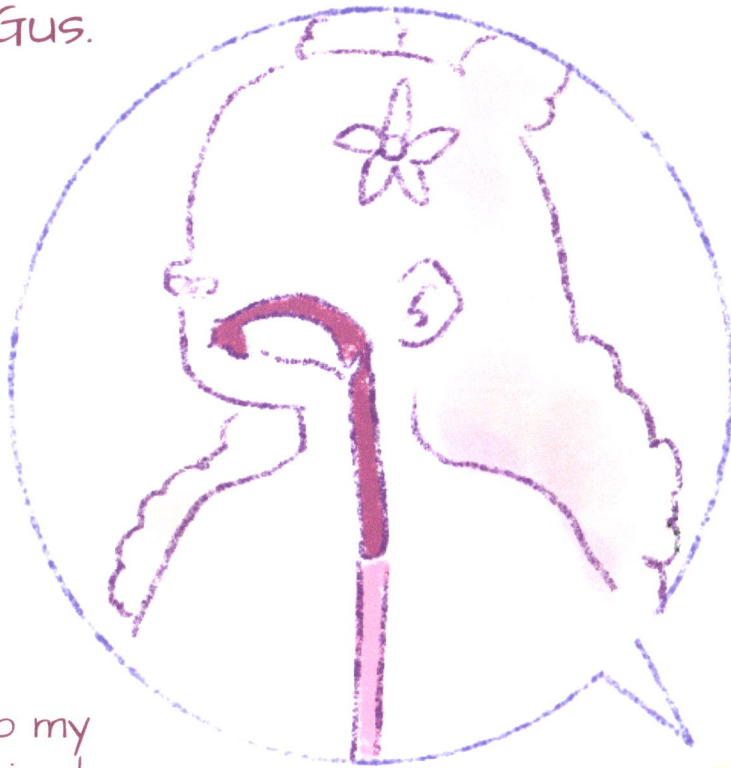

The food goes to my stomach and is mixed up.
Then it goes to my small intestines. The liver and pancreas help me digest the food. Then the food moves to the large intestines, or colon before it comes out of the rectum into the toilet as a bowel movement.

You should read "Do You Know Where My Food Goes?" It's super cool.

Journie: "Now here is where it gets interesting"

You know how mom has a baby in her belly? Well, our little brother or sister is actually in her uterus.

The baby is connected to the uterus by an organ called the placenta, which feeds the baby oxygen, vitamins, and other nutrition.

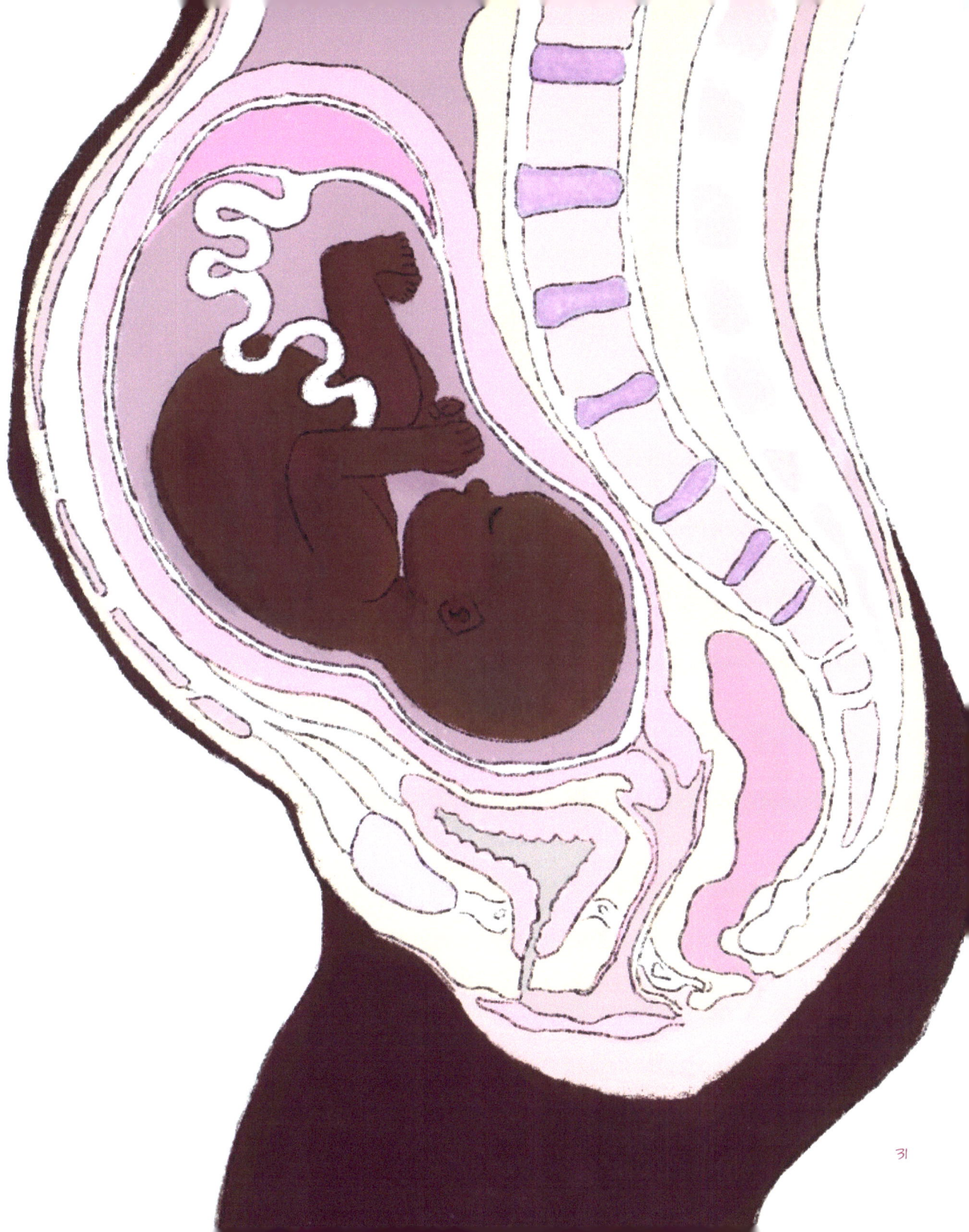

The uterus is between the bladder and the colon/rectum.

Mom always has to go to the bathroom because the uterus becomes large when there is a baby inside. The large uterus pushes on the bladder so it doesn't hold as much urine.

The round ligaments can sometimes hurt. When mom gets up suddenly and feels pain on her side, sometimes that's because of the round ligaments.

The urine comes from our kidneys, which clean the blood and pull out waste and water. The urine collects in the bladder and comes out of the urethra. When people say they "pee," that's called urination.

Behind the urethra is the vagina, and behind the vagina is the rectum. That's where bowel movements come out after going through the digestive system.

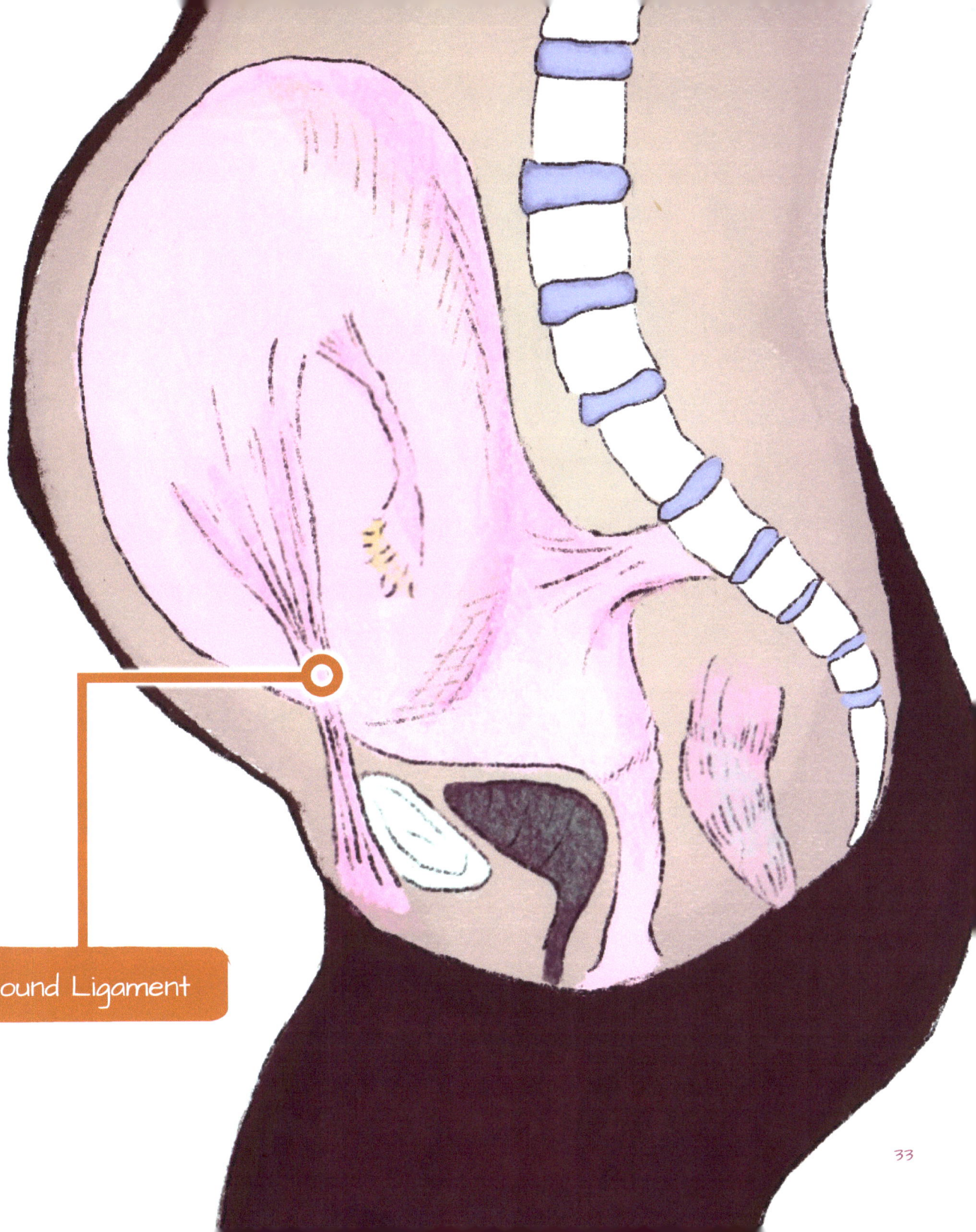

Round Ligament

Look how different everything looks when the uterus doesn't have a baby in it.

Now you can clearly see how much space the uterus, bladder, and rectum take up without pregnancy.

The ovaries and fallopian tubes are on both sides of the uterus.

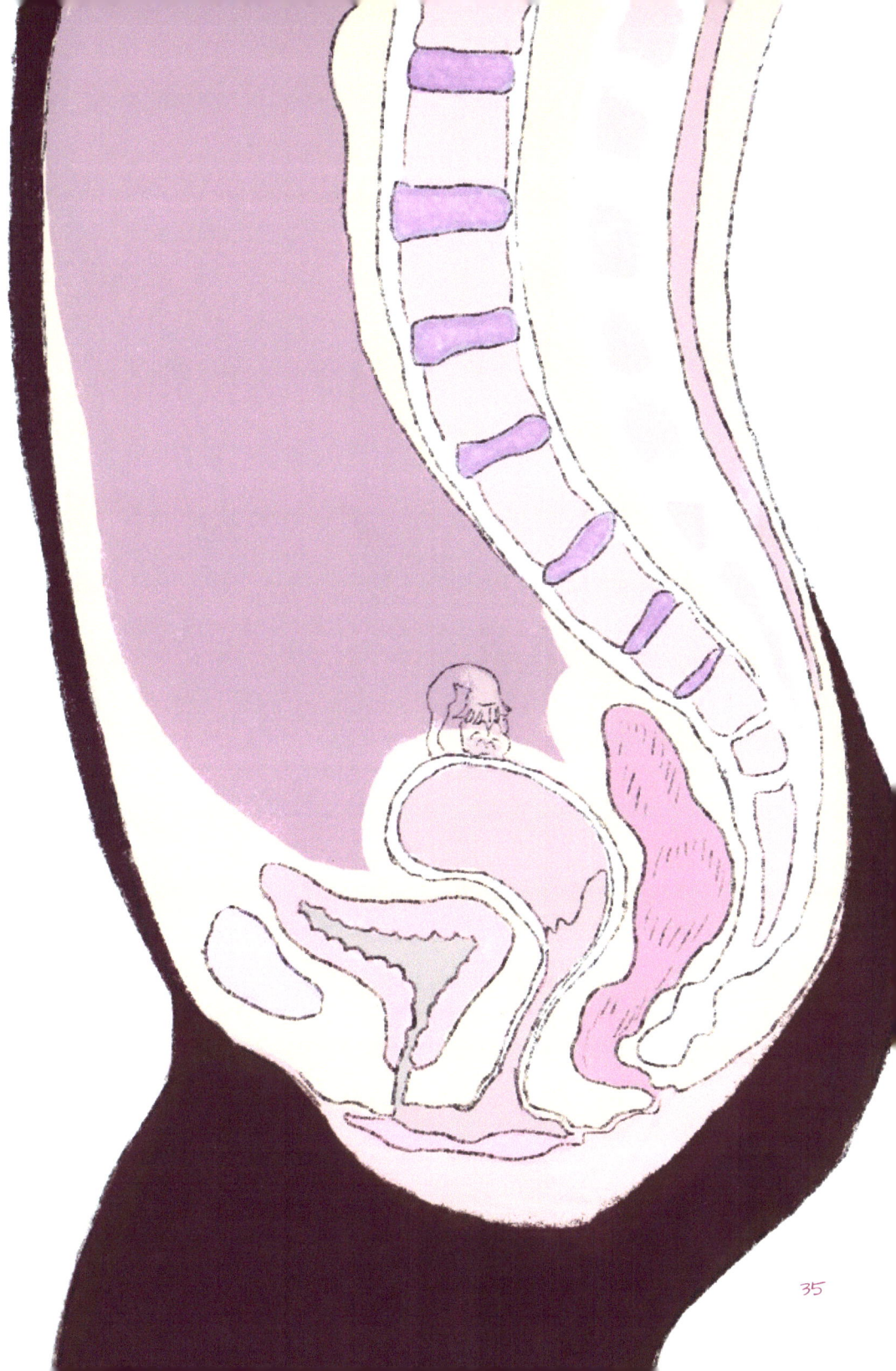

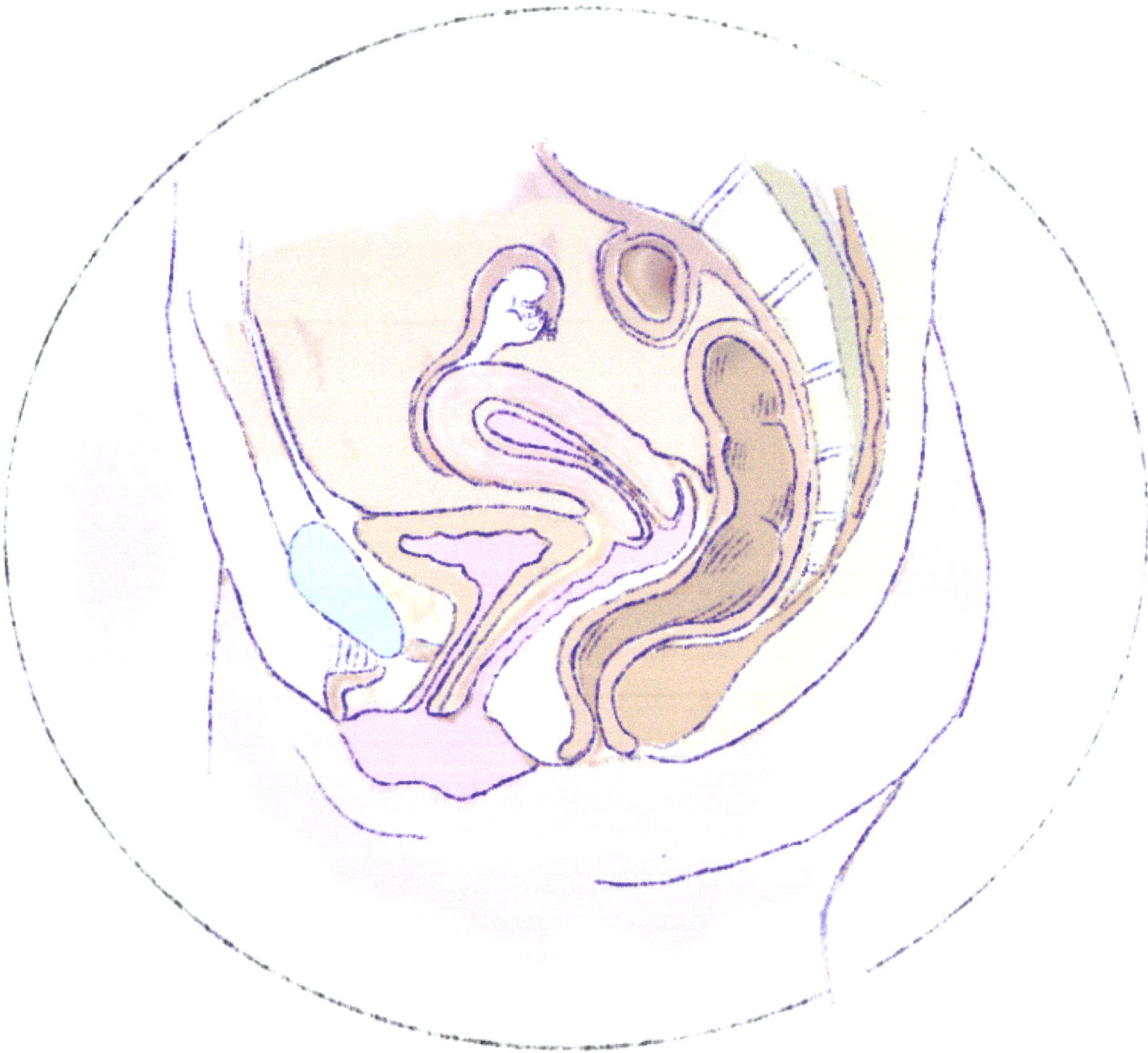

Some people have a uterus,
ovaries, and a vagina.

Some people have a penis and testicles.

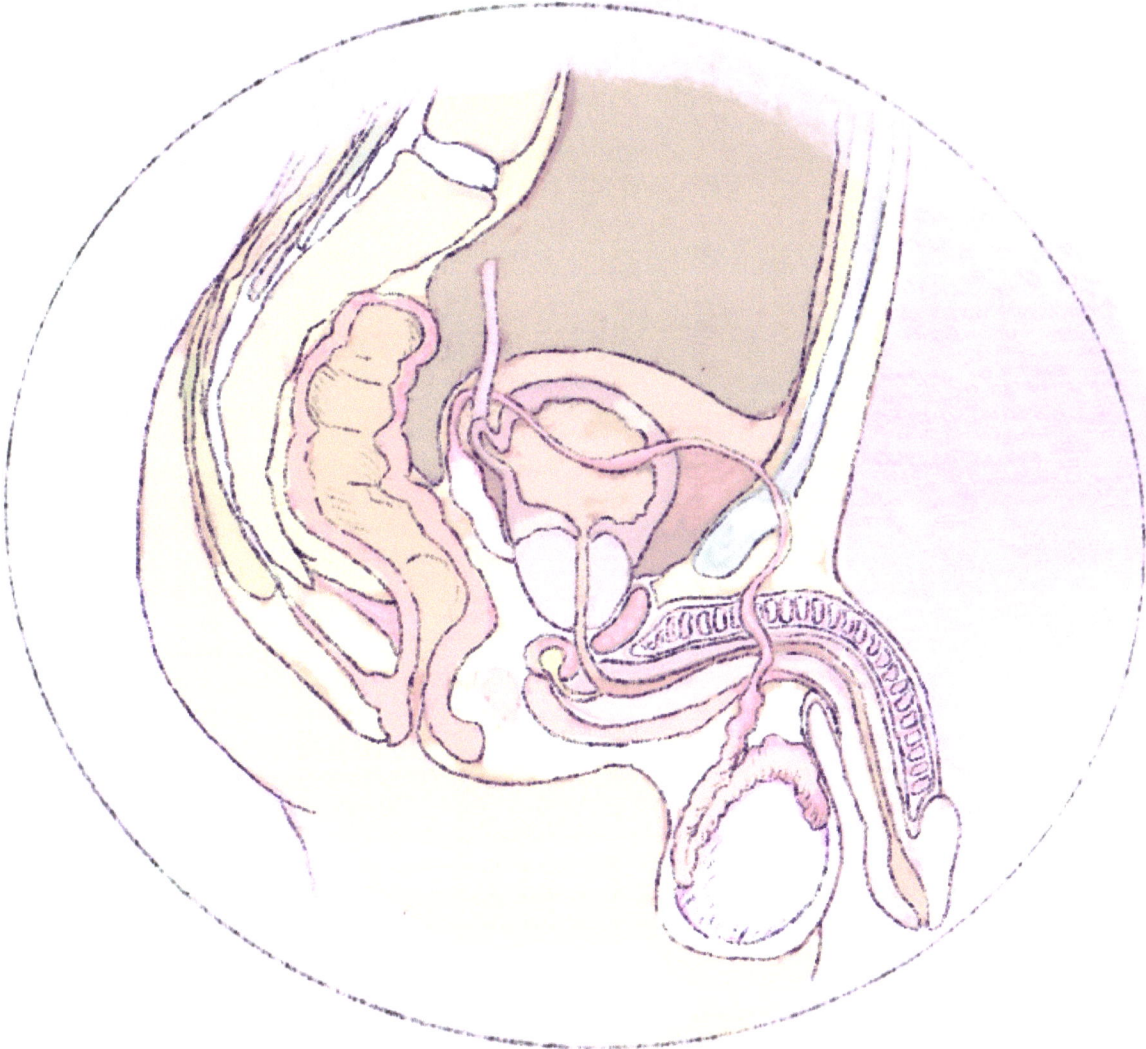

Fun fact: Urine always comes out of the urethra, but the location of the urethra is different depending on which reproductive organs a person has.

Another fun fact: Ovaries and testicles fall under the same category of organs called gonads. While we are being formed in the uterus, the ovaries and testicles start from the same tissue. A signal comes from our genes or chromosomes to determine which organ is formed.

Breasts are another interesting part of anatomy. They contain fat, connective tissue and tiny organs called glands. Those glands can make milk if needed.

Breasts change size and shape when a young person goes through puberty. That usually happens between the ages of 10 and 16.

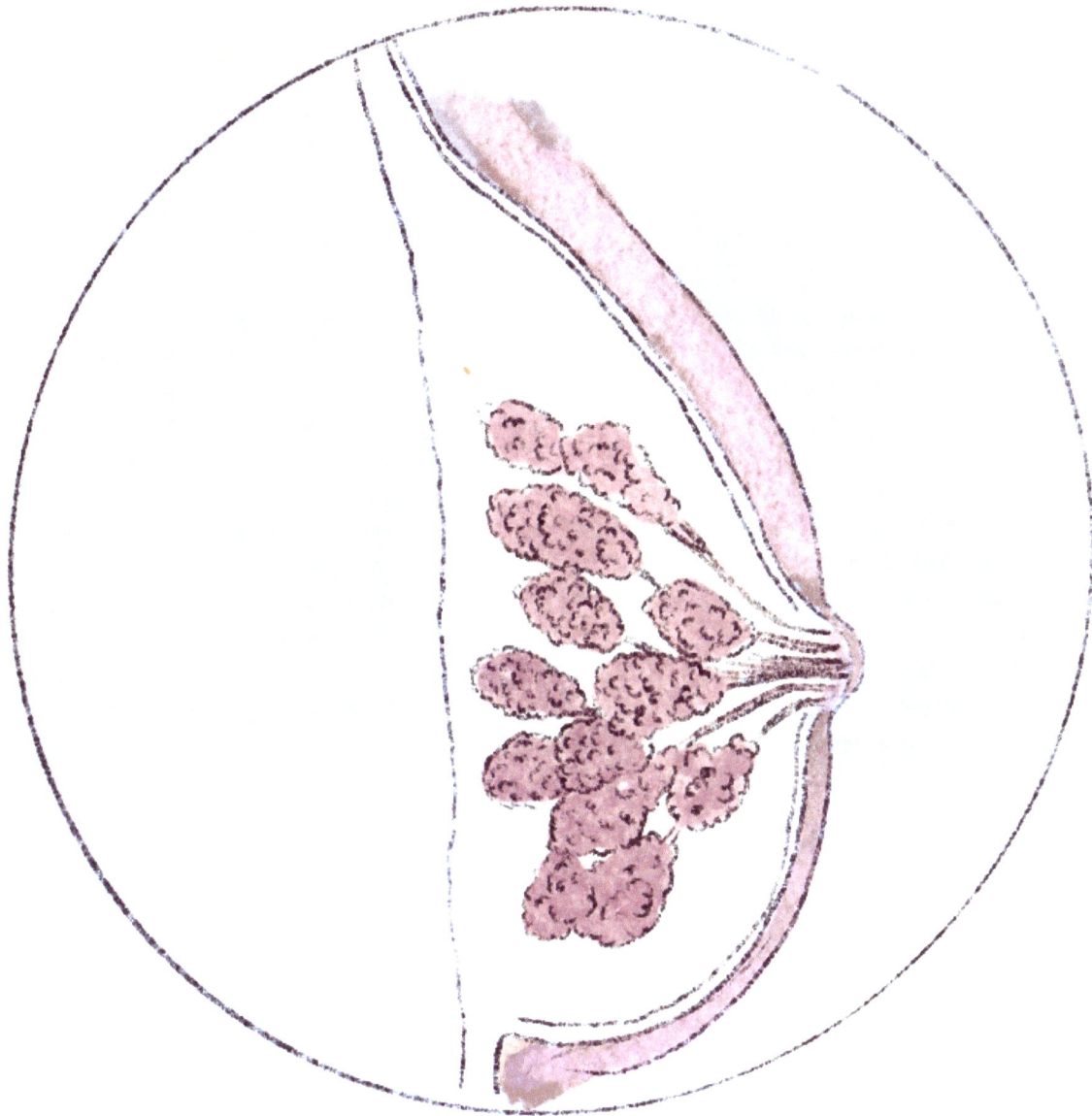

Breasts also change during pregnancy.
Those glands act like little factories making
food for a baby when it's time.

"Whoa, the human body is so complex and magical," said Miles

Yeah, and this is only the tip of the iceberg.

"I think that it is so cool that you are interested in understanding the body that you live in," said Mom.

I love learning about the human body and how I was formed. Maybe one day I'll be just like you and help people take care of the bodies they live in.